MAD about

ART

JUDITH HENEGHAN

WAYLAND

WAYLAND

Published in paperback in 2016 by Wayland
Copyright © Wayland 2016

Wayland, an imprint of
Hachette Children's Group
Part of Hodder & Stoughton
Carmelite House, 50 Victoria Embankment
London EC4Y oDZ

Editor: Nicola Edwards
Design: Rocket Design (East Anglia) Ltd

A catalogue record for this title is available
from the British Library.

ISBN: 978 0 7502 9453 9
Library e-book ISBN: 978 0 7502 8835 4
Dewey number: 702.8-dc23

Printed in China

10 9 8 7 6 5 4 3 2 1

MIX
Paper from
responsible sources
FSC
www.fsc.org   FSC® C104740

Wayland is a division of
Hachette Children's Group,
an Hachette UK company

The author and publisher would like to thank the following for allowing their pictures to be reproduced in this publication: Cover: all Shutterstock; p4 (t) Shutterstock.com/Lucky Business, (b) Getty Images/Sisse Brimberg / National Geographic; p5 (t) Shutterstock.com/Alena Hovorkova, (b) Shutterstock.com/lev radin; p6 (t) Shutterstock.com/OlgAlt, (b) Shutterstock.com/Anna Jurkovska; p7 (t) Mondadori via Getty Images, (b); Shutterstock.com/Melica; p8 (t) Getty Images/Kidstock; (b) Shutterstock.com/uspenskaya; p9 (t) Shutterstock.com/vlastas, (b) Shutterstock.com/BC04; p10 (t) Shutterstock.com/3Art, (bl and br) Shutterstock.com/Aman Ahmed Khan; p11 Shutterstock.com/martan; p12 (t) Shutterstock.com/Stephen Orsillo, (b) Shutterstock.com/Kirill_M; p13 (t) Shutterstock.com/tarasov; (b) Shutterstock.com/Zoom Team; p14 Shutterstock.com/stval; p15 (l) Getty Images/Andreas Kuehn, (r) Wikimedia Commons/epSos. de ; p16 (t) Shutterstock.com/Albachiaraa, (b) Shutterstock.com/kuznetcov_konstantin; p17 (t) Shutterstock.com/Jane Rix, (b) Shutterstock.com/Zadodskov Anatolly Nikolaevich; p18 (t) Shutterstock.com/photka, (b) Shutterstock.com/; p19 (tl), Shutterstock.com/Angie Makes, (tr) Shutterstock.com/camilla$$, (b) Shutterstock.com/Anneka; p20 Wikimedia Commons; p21 (t) Wikimedia Commons, (b) artroom104.blogspot.co.uk; p22 (t) Shutterstock.com/Tumar, (b) Luis Acosta/AFP/Getty Images; p23 (t) Shutterstock.com/ ErickN, (b) Shutterstock.com/ fritz16; p24 (t) Michelle Reader, (b) Shutterstock.com/Jacek Chabraszewski; p25 (t) Shutterstock.com/Sean Donohue Photo, (b) Shutterstock.com/Chris Harvey ; p26 (t) Shutterstock.com/Happy person, (b) Ben Stansall/AFP/Getty Images; p27 (t) VanderWolf Images/Shutterstock.com, (b) Shutterstock.com/carballo; p28 (t) Shutterstock.com/Monkey Business Images, (b) Shutterstock.com/Piotr Majka; p29 (t) Shutterstock.com/buttet, (b) Shutterstock.com/Poznyakov

Every effort has been made to trace the copyright holders. We apologise in advance for any unintentional omissions and would be pleased to insert the appropriate acknowledgements in any future editions of this publication.

Contents

Starting out

Art is brilliant — there are so many things you can do! Today I've sketched my dream fun park, mixed some crazy colours and made cut-out figures from old newspapers. Next I think I'll paint a big jungle scene. I'm always looking out for interesting shapes and patterns. I get my ideas from everywhere.

Express yourself

People have been making art for thousands of years. It is a powerful way to communicate, using shape, colour, line and texture. The art you make can tell a story, show your personality or simply reflect your mood. It can come from your imagination, or the world around you. Anyone can do it, so use this book to have a go. Express yourself!

Humans made these cave paintings in France more than 17,000 years ago.

Use a sketchbook

Not sure where to start? Find a small notebook and use it for scribbles and sketches of anything interesting. It might be something you see — a shape of a leaf or the colours of a sunset. Or it might be something you've found — a feather or a brightly coloured sweet wrapper. Maybe you'll use it to jot down an idea. Keep it with you all the time — you never know when inspiration will strike!

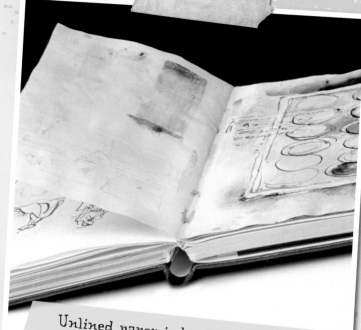

Unlined paper is best for a sketchbook. A hard cover will help keep your ideas safe.

top ★ tip

Remember that it's okay to make mistakes in your sketchbook. It's an ideas book, a place to experiment. That's how great art starts!

THE EXPERT SAYS...

The artist Picasso once said: *"Bad artists copy. Good artists steal."* All artists learn from each other. Whenever you see a painting or a drawing you like, ask yourself why you like it. Visit an art gallery or look at pictures and sculptures on the Internet. Then try creating your own version of your favourite artist's style. It's a great way to pick up tips.

Making marks

I used to be nervous about drawing. Then Dad said that drawing is just making a mark. Now I draw all the time, with a pencil and paper, or a stick in wet sand, or my finger on a steamed-up window or a piece of chalk on the wall outside my house. My sister draws faces in her porridge!

Get confident

Doodling is a great way to gain confidence with drawing. Take a favourite pen or pencil in any colour and let it wander about the paper, making marks. Don't think too much about what you are drawing — just aim to cover the whole page.

Or maybe you prefer to draw familiar objects using simple outline shapes. A cookie or a bicycle wheel is a circle. A mobile phone is a rectangle. Once you have the basic outline in place you can start to fill in the details.

Chalks are great for making quick, colourful marks.

THE EXPERT SAYS...

Paul Klee, a famous artist, one of whose works is shown here, said that *"drawing is like taking a line for a walk"*. You might have some idea about where you are headed, but there are lots of different ways to get there!

Pencil drawing

A pencil is a useful tool for making marks. Find one that is quite soft — 2B or 3B rather than HB — and see what different kinds of marks you can make with it on a sheet of paper. Use the point for lines, pressing harder or lighter to see how this alters the result. Try angling the pencil for soft shaded areas. You can also use a rubber to rub away some of the shading for a different effect.

top tip

Try drawing with charcoal instead of a pencil. Charcoal smudges easily, but you can rub it with your thumb to create interesting shadowy areas on the paper.

What do you see?

Most of the time I draw things I can see. When I start looking around for something to draw, everything becomes interesting: my old trainers, the kitchen taps, our dog asleep in her basket. I draw the basic shapes quickly, with a pencil – just a few lines. Then I can go back and work on it some more if I want to.

Spend time looking at the object you are drawing.

Looking and seeing

Art is about looking and seeing. You'll find yourself thinking about shapes, lines, textures and colours, but that's not all. Artists also look closely at light and shade and the space around and between things. Think of a tree. You can draw twigs and branches. Or you can draw the shapes between the twigs and the branches!

Still life

Sometimes artists deliberately put a few objects together to create an interesting arrangement, or composition. This is called a 'still life'. The artist draws the separate items, but what matters most is the overall effect. Have a go yourself by choosing three pieces of sports kit or items from a kitchen cupboard and grouping them at different angles until you find the most interesting arrangement.

Now get drawing!

top ★ tip

Sometimes the things I want to draw won't stay still. I've been trying to draw the little robin that visits my windowsill for ages. There's an easy solution, though. Take a photo! I can look at the photo to make sure the details in my drawing are just right.

THE EXPERT SAYS...

The artist Vincent van Gogh once said: "Art demands constant observation." If you want a realistic look when you are drawing, think about the size of the different shapes in relation to each other. For example:

How wide is a can of beans in relation to its height?
How long is your dog's tail in relation to its body?
How big is your hand in relation to your face?

Light and shade

I am learning to see shapes as more than outlines. When I look at my hand, I see four fingers and a thumb. I also see lots of bumps and ridges, dips and creases. Some parts are in shadow while other parts are shiny where the light reflects off my skin. These details make my hand unique.

Light and shadow show us that this girl's face is not a flat surface.

Depth

The way the light falls on an object reveals its true shape rather than its outline shape. Think of an orange. Its outline is just a circle; it is one-dimensional. But light coming from a particular direction means parts of it are brighter, and parts are in shadow. Now it is a sphere; it has depth; it is three-dimensional. You can show this in a drawing by using light and shade.

Shading

Pencils are good for shading because you can make the shadow lighter or darker, depending on how hard you press. This is good for creating a gradual effect around a curved object such as a cup. If you are using a pen, draw criss-crossed lines to show the shadowy parts. This is called 'cross-hatching'. For dark shadows, draw lots of lines very close together. For softer shadows, draw the lines further apart. The hand on the opposite page shows you how. Give it a go!

This drawing shows us that light is shining on the apple from the top left.

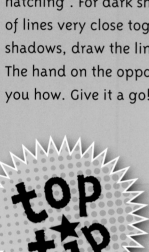

top ★ tip

Showing light

Put a coloured glass bottle on the table and look at where the light is reflected most brightly. Often, the brightest part looks white. You can show this by leaving that part of your drawing blank or rubbing out any shading with a rubber.

CHECKLIST

How to highlight

- ☑ Choose an object to draw.
- ☑ Lightly sketch its outline shape.
- ☑ Look carefully for the light and dark areas.
- ☑ Fill in darker areas using shading or cross-hatching.
- ☑ Use a rubber to highlight the very brightest areas.

Near and far

When I look out of the window, things in the distance appear smaller, while things that are close up appear larger. Showing this in a drawing is called perspective. Perspective adds depth to my pictures and makes them look more realistic.

When you stand at the bottom of a tall building and look up, what happens to the vertical lines?

THE EXPERT SAYS...

One of the first artists to use perspective in painting, Paolo Uccello, said: *"What a delightful thing this perspective is!"* It's fun to play around with perspective. For example, you could make tiny models of people and put them on ordinary sized objects like a loaf of bread or a tree branch and photograph them.

Foreground and background

Most people's feet are bigger than their hands. But when you hold your hand near your face, it looks much bigger than your foot! When you draw a picture, make sure things that are in the front of the picture — the 'foreground' — are bigger than similar objects in the distance — the 'background'.

The road, the grass and the line of trees all head towards the vanishing point.

The vanishing point

If things get smaller as they get further away, at some point they must vanish, right?

Imagine a long straight road, disappearing into the distance. The point at which it becomes too small to see is known as the vanishing point. Now imagine a row of similar-sized houses along one side of the road. Draw a line from the roof of the first house to the vanishing point. All the other houses along the road must fit under this line. The vanishing point helps you work out how much smaller things need to be.

Drawing people

Drawing people is fun because there is so much variety! No two people look the same. I love drawing my gran because she wears big earrings and has loads of curly silver hair and interesting wrinkles. She won't stay still for long though, so sometimes I sit in front of the mirror and draw myself. It's a great way to practise tricky bits like noses and arms.

In proportion

Whatever your size, most people's bodies follow the same proportions, as the picture on the right shows. For example, the body of an adult is usually about seven to eight head-lengths. A baby's body is three to four head-lengths (they have big heads!). It's a good idea to make light pencil marks to check proportions before you start filling in the detail.

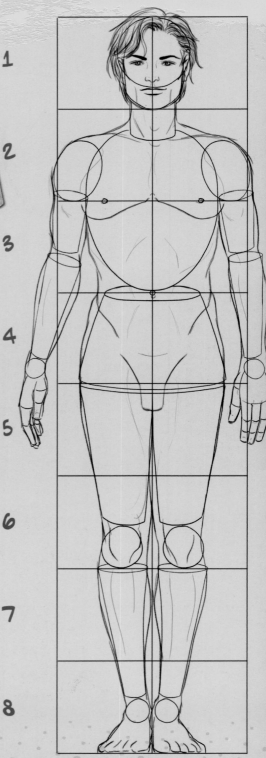

1
2
3
4
5
6
7
8

Try drawing a friend or relative while they are asleep! They should stay still long enough for you to capture plenty of interesting detail. Another useful tip is to draw someone from a photograph. Don't forget to give your drawing some light and shade.

What's your angle?

The human body is full of joints and muscles all designed to help us move in lots of interesting ways. Try drawing a person at an unusual angle, with their arms doing different things or their head turned or their legs crossed. This will look more natural and it'll give your drawing more personality.

CHECKLIST

☑ Your hand is usually the same size as your face.

☑ Your foot is usually the same size as your forearm from elbow to wrist.

☑ Eyes are usually halfway down your head.

If you're not sure, check!

Using colour

I can't imagine a world without colour! It brings my art to life. Felt-tips or coloured pencils are quick and easy to use, but most of the time I like to paint with lots of strong, bold colour mixed in interesting combinations. I mix the colour on a plate and test it on some scrap paper before I add it to my painting.

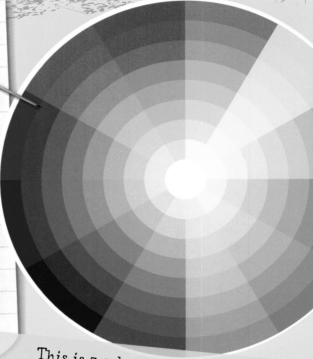

This is a colour wheel. Colours that are opposite each other create contrast and balance in a painting.

Primary colours

There are thousands of different colours, but only three 'primary' colours — red, yellow and blue. Every other colour is a mix of these three. You probably know that mixing red and blue makes purple, mixing red and yellow makes orange and mixing blue and yellow makes green. But what if you add a tiny amount of blue to red and yellow, or a tiny amount of yellow to blue and red? How many different colours can you make?

Tone

Tone is how light or dark a colour is. Different tones of the same colour are more interesting than a single tone — they create light and shade in a picture, and add depth. Adding white to a colour will lighten its tone, while adding black will darken it. For more variation, try using a little yellow as a lightener, or some blue to make your colours darker.

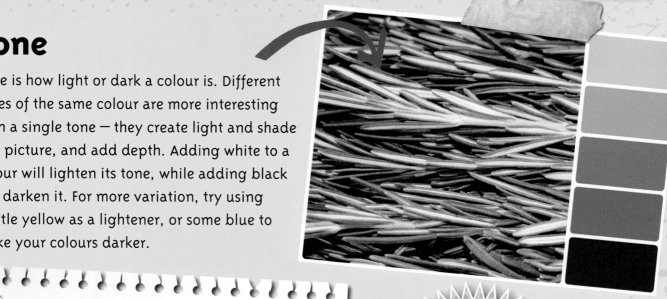

CHECKLIST

Here are some brilliant things to do with colour:

- ☑ face-painting
- ☑ tie-dying t-shirts
- ☑ decorating cakes with bright food dyes
- ☑ finger painting
- ☑ painting hard-boiled eggs
- ☑ potato-print making

top tip

You can create different types of white by mixing in tiny amounts of other colours.

Look at something white such as a tea cup or a white sock. Is it pure white, or can you see some blue or grey or creamy-yellow tints?

Try painting a snow scene using lots of different tones and tints of white.

Painting techniques

Today I'm painting a jungle scene with lots of leafy plants and animals watching from the trees. I sketched it out in pencil first, then painted the background colours. Now I'm working on the details, using oil pastels to highlight some things and a smudge of charcoal for the really dark bits. Using different materials like this is called 'mixed media'.

top tip

Using an easel

An easel is a stand for your paper or canvas. It allows you to paint or draw at a more natural angle. Easels are great if you are painting or drawing something from real life, because you don't have to keep looking down to see what you are doing. Just be careful your paint doesn't run!

Watercolour

Watercolour paints are blocks or tubes of paint that dissolve easily in water. The colours are meant to be quite diluted and watery. This means that when you brush the paint onto your paper the colours run and blend into each other, creating interesting effects. It's best to use a paintbrush with long, soft bristles that hold the water for longer.

You can use watercolours to paint a background wash, let it dry, then add more detail.

CHECKLIST

Ways to colour:

☑ Watercolours – big washes of soft colour and light, delicate detail

☑ Water-based acrylics – bright, bold, dry quite quickly

☑ Oil paints – thick, slow-drying, use on canvas, quite expensive

☑ Oil pastels – like crayons but smoother, richer, better for blending

☑ Watercolour pencils – pale colour, use like a pencil for detail but can also brush with water for softer effect.

Oils and acrylics

Oil paints are thicker and heavier than watercolour. They are used on canvas, which is stronger than paper. Any oil-based paint takes weeks to dry, which means you can work on a painting over a long period of time, building up layers of colour and texture. Water-based acrylic paints are a cheaper and easier alternative. They dry more quickly but you can still use thick, bold dabs of colour.

19

Create an impression

In my jungle painting I have painted a pool of water using little streaks of colour. Some streaks are blue, some are green, some are dark purple-brown and a few are yellowy-white. I want it to look like the water is swirling and deep. I think I've created the right impression!

Colour and mood

Many artists use colour in interesting ways to create an impression. It may not seem realistic to use bright blue to paint a shadow on a wall, for example, but our brains interpret blue as coolness and shade. Colours create mood and artists use them in all kinds of ways to reflect what they are feeling.

Vincent Van Gogh's 'The Starry Night'

This painting by Georges Seurat uses dots of contrasting colour.

Dabs and dots

You can also use different paint techniques to create an impression. Van Gogh often used thick streaks and dabs of different coloured paint to suggest light or movement. Seurat's paintings, meanwhile, are made up of individual dots of colour. These artists tried to avoid blending different colours; they knew that our brains pick up the separate colours and mix them automatically!

top tip

Make a collage out of torn-up pictures from a magazine, or recycled objects like bottle tops or eggshells, or little blobs of sparkly nail varnish. Think about how the different shapes and colours work together to provide texture and tone and create an overall effect.

This collage made from recycled materials was inspired by Van Gogh's 'The Starry Night'.

Use your imagination

I love making things from my imagination. It might be a painting of somewhere I've never been, like the jungle, or the moon. It might be a model of something fantastical, like a dragon, or a collage of crazy plants or a mysterious underwater world. My art lets me go wild!

Surrealism

Some artists create paintings that contain something unexpected, something that we wouldn't see in the 'real' world. These artists are called 'surrealists'; their aim is to make us ask questions about what we know, or think we know. Salvador Dali was a surrealist painter and one of his most famous paintings shows clocks that look as if they are melting.

Are the men in this painting by René Magritte floating, or raining?

Mask making

People have been making and wearing masks for thousands of years. You can 'become' a person or creature from your imagination. Venice in Italy is famous for its jewelled and painted masks (see right). Try making one of your own by layering torn-up newspaper over a blown-up balloon using PVA glue. Once the glue is dry, cut the hardened shell into a mask shape and decorate!

A mask maker at work.

CHECKLIST

'Papier mache' is French for 'chewed paper'. It's great for making masks. You will need:

- ☑ Lots of newspaper torn up into matchbox-sized pieces
- ☑ A blown-up balloon
- ☑ PVA glue, watered down
- ☑ Paints

Art in 3D

You can make a three-dimensional (3D) model or artwork out of anything. I made a slithering snake out of empty cans and toilet rolls strung together with different coloured wool. It has scales made from silver foil. My mum helped me hang it from the curtain pole in my bedroom. The scales glint in the sunlight!

This duck sculpture is made from recycled materials.

Sculpture

A work of three-dimensional art that is carved or modelled is usually called a sculpture. A sculpture might be carved out of materials like stone or wood or ice or soap, or modelled out of clay or dough or wool or any type of found object such as pieces of scrap metal or recycled materials.

A massive sand sculpture inspired by the nursery rhyme 'There was an old woman who lived in a shoe'.

top ★ tip

If you make something in 3D you'll need to work on it from every angle. Walk around it, look at it from above and below. Does it look interesting all the way around?

Step inside

Some 3D art is created to work within a specific space or location such as a gallery or a park. This kind of art is called an 'installation'. Often you can walk inside it or across it or under it. You might even be expected to touch it. In this way, the viewer becomes part of the artwork!

THE EXPERT SAYS...

Carsten Holler, an artist who designed a huge installation of curving slides at the Tate Modern gallery in London, said that people were both spectators and performers when they visited his work. If you had an empty room and some materials, what kind of installation would you make? How would you want people to experience it?

What does it mean?

Does an artwork have to 'mean' anything?

Sometimes I see a painting or a sculpture and I'm not sure what it is, or what it means. It may not look like anything I recognise. I don't know what to think about it, or even if I like it. But sometimes that's the point of art. It makes me ask questions about it. It makes me react to it. And that's exciting!

Abstract art

Abstract art deliberately avoids representing something in a realistic way. You might decide to paint a blue man, for example, and this would be partly abstract — the man shape might be realistic but the colour is not. Other art is more fully abstract — it has no realistic shape or form. The artist Mark Rothko used large strips of colour to create his paintings. They don't 'look' like anything but many people say they make them feel things.

A visitor looks at 'Black on Maroon' by Mark Rothko. The painting was restored after it was vandalised in 2012.

Art with a message

On the other hand, some artists create work that has a very clear message. They want to make a point. In the twentieth century, artists like Pablo Picasso and Diego Rivera created large paintings and murals (wall paintings) to make people think about the effects of war or poverty. A British artist called Banksy has become famous for his graffiti-style art on the sides of buildings that makes fun of the way we behave and the things we take for granted.

This graffiti art by Banksy shows a young girl and a soldier. What do you think it is trying to say?

top tip

To create an abstract painting that expresses something about you, paint a picture using colours, but without using any 'realistic' shapes.

THE EXPERT SAYS...

Pablo Picasso said: "I paint objects as I think them, not as I see them." He didn't rely on realistic images; instead he thought about what he wanted to show and used his imagination.

Express yourself

Me and my friends are putting on an art exhibition at our youth club. We're using one room as a studio where we made all the artwork. Now we've got to decide how to display everything — we want it to feel like an art gallery. We're going to invite our friends and family to a grand opening.

Art can be fast and buzzy, or slow and relaxed.

Do your own thing

Whether you are doing quick doodles, painting a big picture or putting on an exhibition for others to view, the most important thing is that you are expressing something about you. Take inspiration from other artists, learn some skills but above all do your own thing.

The street artist Banksy says that *"bus stops are far more interesting and useful places to have art than in museums"*. Going to an art gallery is an amazing experience, but don't forget that art is all around you. Think about the cover art for your favourite book, or a fabric design you like. There is so much to look at and be inspired by: nature, people, buildings, food. Keep that sketchbook handy. Use it as often as you can!

Frame it

A frame can help show off your artwork. Try a simple frame made of coloured paper or cardboard. Or decorate your frame with gold paint or shells or glitter. A fancy frame can be part of the fun!

top tip

Perhaps you've made a picture or a sculpture that you are particularly proud of. Why not display it for others to see? You might decide to make a frame for your painting. Give your artwork a title and make sure you sign it. Your signature tells people it is your unique creation.

Quiz

How mad about art are you? Try this quiz and find out!

1. Red, yellow and blue are called primary colours because:

(a) they are at the top of all the colour charts;

(b) they are the three colours from which all other colours are made;

(c) they are the most frequently used colours.

2. 'Mixed media' artwork consists of the following:

(a) a variety of different materials including charcoal, paint, pastel and inks;

(b) newspapers, magazines and advertisements;

(c) recycled objects.

3. When you are making a realistic drawing of a person's face, the eyes should go in which position?

(a) one third of the way down the face;

(b) 10 cm either side of the nose;

(c) about half way down the head.

4. Some painters are called 'impressionists' because:

(a) they can do funny voices;

(b) their paintings are done very quickly;

(c) they use dabs of colour that create an impression of light and movement.

5. What type of pencil is best for drawing?

(a) 6X

(b) 2B

(c) HHB

6. What kind of art is 'surrealist' art?

(a) art that shows something that isn't possible in the 'real' world;

(b) art that uses unrealistic colours;

(c) art that no one can understand.

7. An artist can suggest distance in a painting in the following ways:

(a) by making objects in the distance look darker;

(b) by making objects in the distance look more yellow;

(c) by making objects in the distance look smaller and paler than objects in the foreground.

8. What kind of art is an installation?

(a) a sculpture made from household objects;

(b) a large, three-dimensional artwork designed for a specific site;

(c) a type of mural, or wall painting.

Answers:
1(b); 2(a); 3(c); 4(c); 5(b); 6(a); 7(c); 8(b)

Glossary

abstract art Art that doesn't use recognisable shapes or forms.

acrylic paint Thick, bright paint — usually water-based.

art gallery A place where you can see an artist's work.

background The part of a picture showing what's in the distance.

canvas A hard-wearing material used instead of paper for oil paintings.

charcoal Black, smudgy drawing material.

collage A picture made from things stuck onto the paper.

colour wheel A way of arranging colours to show neighbouring and contrasting shades.

contrasting colours Colours on opposite sides of the colour wheel.

cross-hatching Fine lines criss-crossing each other to create a shaded effect.

easel A stand for holding a painting or drawing.

foreground The nearest things in a picture.

impressionist Describes an art style where colour and brush strokes create the illusion of light or movement.

installation A large sculpture that is created for a particular space; often interactive.

mixed media Using different kinds of paint, pencil, pastel or ink in a single painting.

oil paint Thick, slow drying paint that can't be mixed with water.

oil pastels Oily, crayon-like sticks of colour.

one-dimensional Flat and having no depth — like a simple drawing of a circle.

papier mache A modelling material made from torn-up paper and glue.

perspective Showing how things in the distance look smaller, according to how far away they are.

primary colours Red, blue and yellow; the colours from which all others are made.

PVA glue Glue that is suitable for sticking paper or cardboard; it can be mixed with water and it hardens when dry.

realistic art Art that aims, as far as possible, to look like something real.

scale The size of something in relation to something else.

sculpture A three-dimensional artwork that is carved or modelled.

sketchbook A book with blank pages for sketches and notes.

surrealists Artists who combine realistic images with something unreal to create a visual surprise.

three-dimensional Something that has height, width and depth.

tone The amount of light or dark in a colour.

vanishing point The point at which an object becomes too far away to see.

watercolour Paints that dissolve in water to create soft, pale washes of colour.

Index